IN SUNSHINE OR IN SHA

GW00792950

To Gladys and Evy

First published 1990
Friar's Bush Press
24 College Park Avenue
BELFAST BT7 1LR
© David Bigger and Terence McDonald

This book has received financial support from the Cultural Traditions programme of the Community Relations Council which aims to encourage acceptance and understanding of cultural diversity.

ISBN 0 946872 36 8

Designed by Rodney Miller Associates
Printed by W. & G. Baird Ltd, Antrim

Front cover: Strand Road
Back cover: Departing family

IN SUNSHINE OR IN SHADOW

Photographs from the Derry Standard, 1928-39

David Bigger and Terence McDonald

Introduction by Brian M. Walker

FRIAR'S BUSH PRESS

INTRODUCTION

This book is a very special achievement. In part, its unique quality arises from the rarity of the type of photographic record on which it is based and the excellence of the actual photographs. More importantly, the book reflects the remarkable efforts of the compilers of the material, David Bigger and Terence McDonald. They saved the original glass negatives from destruction in 1968, and have worked painstakingly on the collection ever since, conserving, cataloguing and researching the photographs. They have brought to this task their extensive local knowledge. The end result is a striking view of life in the decade before the outbreak of the second world war.

The *Derry Standard* was founded in 1836 and ran until its closure in 1966. It adopted the use of photographs on its pages in the mid 1920s. Unfortunately our knowledge of the identity of the paper's early photographers is scanty. It is reputed that the first photographer was a Mr Lackner, who was of European origins. He was also employed by the paper as a process engraver, that is the person responsible for making from the photographs the zinc plates which were used for printing. In the late 1930s Baxter Robinson replaced Lackner. Two years after the newspaper closed, the bulk of the photographic records, consisting of an enormous total of over 14,000 quarter plate glass negatives were rescued by David Bigger and Terence McDonald. Although at this last stage some negatives were thrown out, before they would be saved, the survival of the remainder is of great importance, not only because few photographs remain from the city's other newspapers for this pre-war period, but also because no major newspaper photographic archive for this decade has survived anywhere else in Northern Ireland, or indeed in the rest of Ireland.

In the years which followed their acquisition, David Bigger and Terence McDonald exerted remarkable energy and skill in cleaning and conserving this large collection of fragile glass negatives. In addition they researched the material, a task made difficult because of the destruction by a bomb and fire of the city's main library at Gwynn's Institute, Brooke Park, where the original copies of the *Derry Standard* were stored: six of the volumes for the 1930s were burnt. Over the years a number of exhibitions of the photographs were mounted and in 1989 a whole programme in the B.B.C. television series *Northern Lights* on Ulster photographers, written by Kieran Hickey and myself, was devoted to this collection, because of its special quality. Now for the first time, a major volume contains a wide range of this material, selected, and with captions, by David Bigger and Terence McDonald. A few of the prints chosen do show some signs of marking or wear but most are in good condition.

These photographs give a fascinating view of Londonderry and its people before the second world war. As little changed physically between 1939 and the late 1960, they record strikingly the buildings and streetscape of the city before the destruction of the last two decades. They capture the vitality of the people who inhabited this community. As the title implies, the photographs show not just the happy times, as seen in the dances and sporting events, but also the unhappy times, as glimpsed in some of the haunting photographs of the emigrants. Compared to the expanding, highly prosperous late Victorian and Edwardian eras, the 1920s and 1930s were less successful. Closure of the shipyards and Watts distillery in the early 1920s damaged employment prospects in the city. Partition in 1921 had little effect on the economic and social life of the city (the border at this stage was primarily a political boundary), but the economic war between the Free State and the U.K. in the 1930s restricted links between Derry and its Donegal hinterland. Yet, in spite of these difficulties, the city, in its numerous factories, shops and offices, continued to supply employment for thousands of its citizens: its many schools, hospitals, societies and churches continued to look after the varied needs of the community.

Altogether these photographs give a unique picture of life in Derry in these years. They show a robust city which, in spite of divisive political problems and economic difficulties, faced the world with spirit and style. The strong cultural heritage of the community, which embraced a wide range of religious and ethnic diversities, and which gave the city special character and quality, is shown well in these pages. Whether called Derry or Londonderry, the city illustrated in this book emerges as a vibrant, living entity. David Bigger and Terence McDonald, in rescuing the material from oblivion and giving us a striking visual record of our past, have left us all greatly in their debt.

Brian M. Walker
Deputy-director, The Institute of Irish Studies,
The Queen's University of Belfast.

CONTENTS

CONTENTS

Although S.S. *Lairdsburn* was not one of the regular Burns and Laird Line vessels which plied between Derry and Glasgow, she was typical of those that did, and is pictured here in August 1939 leaving the port with a full complement of passengers, especially in the steerage class. The passenger steamship service between the two ports ended in the autumn of 1966 when the *Lairds Loch* was transferred to the Dublin-Glasgow route. After 1966 steamers continued to carry cargo livestock for a short time.

Even in the 1930s the occasional sailing ship entered the port and attracted some interest, as is shown here at Princes Quay which still had a wooden planked surface. The bollard shows quite an amount of wear. The caption which accompanied this photograph in the *Derry Standard* on 11th April 1932 was, *A three masted schooner at Derry Quay with a cargo of ice. This type of vessel is rapidly disappearing.*

SKULDA

Some idea of the employment that the port provided may be gleaned from this photograph of a consignment of wood being unloaded for either Robert Keys or J. & J. Ballantine at Queen's Quay. The number of men engaged working at the forward hold appears to be sixteen, and presumeably a similar number was employed at the stern of the vessel.

A scene at Queen's Quay shows the sheds which were a feature of the riverside. Also in this photograph is the tramway rail track which can accommodate standard or narrow gauge rolling stock, and a reminder that there were sailings to Heysham. These catered for passenger traffic and cargo/livestock up to 1930 when the former ceased: the latter continued up to October 1963.

During the 1930s there were periodic visits for training purposes by R.A.F. Supermarine Southampton Flying Boats: one of which is shown here landing on the river with Ebrington Barracks in the background. The tall chimney was that belonging to Ebrington Factory which was reduced in height at the outbreak of 1939-45 War.

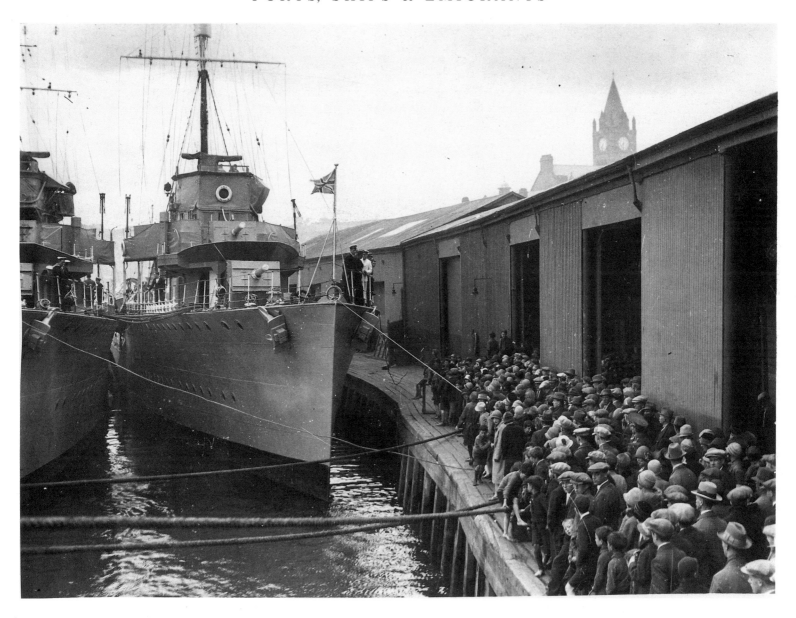

When naval vessels visited the port between the wars one of the attractions for the townspeople was the chance to inspect the ships. Judging by the number of people waiting to board the craft in this early 1930s scene at Queen's Quay, the crews would have been fully employed for a few hours.

P.S. *Cynthia* leaving its berth at Abercorn Quay on what appears to be an excursion trip, as there is a brass band on board. The *Cynthia* came to the port when she was fifteen years old in 1907 and remained here until c.1930 after which she specialised in local cruises at Bangor. In November 1931 she was purchased by A.H. Hewitt of Dublin who used her as a liner tender for the 1932 Eucharistic Congress at Dublin. During a storm in early 1933 the *Cynthia* broke her moorings and foundered. R. L. Praegar, in his autobiography *The way that I went* relates how the vessel was fog-bound overnight with several hundred passengers on board, near Horn Head, in July 1910.

P S *Seamore* was acquired by the Anchor Line in 1928 and acted as the company's tug-tender until 1939 when the transatlantic passenger service liners calling in at Moville ceased. The steamer is shown here leaving its berth which was opposite the bottom of John Street.

Emigration through the port continued up to the start of the second world in 1939. Here a large group of hopefuls pose outside the Anchor Line Offices in Foyle Street before boarding the tender at Abercorn Quay.

A scene which took place on countless occasions just prior to the tender leaving its berth at the Transatlantic shed, Abercorn Quay, to set sail down the Foyle to meet the liners in Moville Bay. This photograph was taken on board the P.S. *Seamore* c.1936-38, judging by the hats worn by the ladies.

A family on board one of the liner tender paddle steamers just before setting off down the river for Moville. The young girl is holding a paper bag containing what appears to be an orange or apple whilst her father is keeping a tight grip of the tickets for the journey in his right hand.

A typical emigrant family on board P.S. *Seamore* about to start a new life in the 'New World'.

A late 1920s scene of the Diamond with newly erected War Memorial, a milk cart plodding its way into Bishop Street past an enormous telegraph pole and Mulholland's shop. On close examination it would appear that every person in it is wearing some type of headgear.

A rather sad scene at the War Memorial c.1928, on the anniversary of the Battle of the Somme on 1st July showing four young girls wearing their fathers' medals.

Sawers shop at the junction of Strand Road/Sackville Street is shown here immediately before it was demolished in 1926, prior to the erection of the National Bank, now part of the Bank of Ireland Group. The bus is one of those operated by the Londonderry Corporation.

A late 1920s scene of Waterloo Place looking towards Shipquay Place when the horse still ruled the roost, but motor vehicles are becoming more numerous. The Ulster Bank, which was damaged by a bomb in the 1970s and subsequently demolished, is shown on the right.

The second operator of the city's bus service was Catherwood, one of whose vehicles is shown in this 1934 scene of Waterloo Place. McCullagh's grocery establishment is aptly named 'The Golden Teapot' whilst to the left of it is J. &. J. Cooke's hardware and sports shop.

The scene in Waterloo Place when Littlewoods opened their 3d to 2/11 store in November 1938.
Policemen are attempting to keep the crowds back from the two right hand entrances of the store.

Sir Robert A. Ferguson was M.P. for the city from 1830 to 1860, and after his death a statue to his memory was placed at the top of Shipquay street where it remained until the late 1920s when the War Memorial was constructed in the Diamond, after which 'The Black Man' was re-erected at the entrance to Brooke Park.

Apart from the man and kid, this scene at the Diamond is interesting as it shows the road surface without tarmacadam and a crossing consisting of granite slabs and square setts. The latter was essential at a time when roads were muddy and women wore long clothes.

The man sitting on the wooden box in Ferryquay Street with a placard on his chest is blind and is begging. Scattered through the main shopping areas there would have been four or five other men in a similar plight who had to resort to this method of supplementing their meagre allowances. At the time this scene was recorded, in the 1930s, Woolworths had still to expand by incorporating the premises of Irvine's Clothiers and Outfitters.

A 1933 traffic jam in Ferryquay Street, in which both horse and motor vehicles are involved, attracted a large crowd of onlookers who paused for a few seconds to look towards the photographer standing on Ferryquay Gate.

A cobbled Foyle Street looking towards the Guildhall, taken from outside Roberts Garage. Buildings line both sides of the street, and on the left is the Melville Hotel which on this occasion appears to be the headquarters of an M.G. Motor car rally. Foyle Street boasted four other hotels during the 1930s - Metropole, Foyle, Provincial and City.

THE CITY CENTRE

This narrow section of Duke Street was the cause of many traffic jams as the number of motor vehicles increased until eventually in the late 1960s a major road scheme resulted in the buildings in this photograph being demolished as far as L.M.S. Railway Station.

25

Clergy processing into St Columb's Cathedral on 18th July 1933 for a service on the occasion of the tercentenary of its founding. The magnificent entrance gates at the top of Pump Street were presented by the Honourable The Irish Society, the builders of the Cathedral, in the same year.

Rev. James Albert Donaldson was installed as minister of Gt James Street Presbyterian Church in 1939. He is seen here on the steps of the church with elders and visiting clergy. The front row consists of Professor Woodburn, President of Magee University College, John Whittington, Rev Donaldson, Wallace Edmiston and R. A. Cunningham,

Magee University College opened in October 1865 as a college for the training of young men for the Presbyterian Church. When this scene was photographed c.1933 there were quite a number of women students and the college catered for non-theology students who completed their degree at Trinity College, Dublin. The person on the right of the back row is Adam Quigley, janitor of the College, who was a stalwart of the hockey team for many years.

The People's Hall, Corporation Street, was run by Clooney Hall Methodist Church. As well as catering for the usual church activities there was a men's hostel attached to the hall. The building was completed in 1933 and the photograph shows the scene on the occasion of the laying of foundation stones.

The Mission Church, at the top of Claremont Street, suitably decorated for a harvest thanksgiving service. The structure was of corrugated iron lined with wood, with gas lighting and heating. The congregation was attached to Christ Church.

A group of children in confirmation dress at St Columb's Wells on 9 June, the patron saint's feast day. The well is dressed with oak leaves which are also worn by some of the children.

The Eucharistic Congress took place in Dublin during June, 1932, and as part of the local celebrations this arch was erected in Rossville Street. Nearby residents are standing proudly beneath it.

A Eucharistic Congress Arch in Fahan Street just below the Little Diamond with nearby residents posing below the structure. In addition to the arch depicted here there were others in Rossville Street, Lecky Road and Stanley's Walk.

Bishop Bernard O'Kane laying the foundation stone of St Patrick's Church, Pennyburn, on 23rd February, 1932. As well as being head of a large diocese Dr O'Kane was held in high regard as a physicist.

Cardinal McRory being welcomed at the city boundary, Victoria Road, on the occasion of his visit to consecrate Dr Neil Farren as Bishop of Derry on 1st October, 1939.

Dr Neil Farren and his two sponsoring bishops processing into St Eugene's Cathedral on 1st October 1939, for his consecration as Bishop of Derry. The altar boy is holding the train of Cardinal McRory.

Bishop Neil Farren outside St Eugene's Cathedral after his consecration as Bishop of Derry on 1st October 1939. On his episcopal ordination he was the youngest prelate on the bench of Irish bishops at the age of 46 years. He resigned his see on the grounds of age in 1973, retired to his native Buncrana, and died on 7th May 1980.

An arch in Wapping Lane erected to celebrate the anniversary of the Relief of Derry on 12th August, 1689. By tradition, when a photograph of such a structure was taken, the persons responsible for its construction, nearby residents and children posed below it. The arch shown here has the various sections outlined with bows made out of dyed wood shavings which were tacked to the framework, and as an additional feature this arch was illuminated by coloured electric light bulbs, the current coming from an adjacent house.

Clarence Place, off Fountain Street, had two murals. The other, at the end of the cul-de-sac, by the late Robert Jackson has been preserved; but this one, along with the houses, disappeared in the Fountain redevelopment scheme.

Scene on the City Walls before the start of a Relief Parade in the mid 1930s. The Walker Memorial has been suitably decorated for the occasion.

The Apprentice Boys' Memorial Hall in Socicty Street during major extensions in the mid 1930s which cost £30,000. The renovated building was re-opened in 1937, and as well as being dedicated to the thirteen apprentices who shut Ferryquay Gate in 1688, the hall is a memorial to those members of the Apprentice Boys who died during the 1st World War.

Matthew Kerr, Governor of the Apprentice Boys of Derry, leads a parade in Carlisle Road. On his right is the Lieut Governor, Alex. Birney. Matt. Kerr had a printing business in London Street whilst his deputy, who was employed in a local bakery, was popularly known as 'Cooky Bun'.

On the 18th December, the anniversary of the shutting of the Gates in 1688, an effigy of Col Lundy was suspended from Walker's Pillar on the City Walls. When darkness fell the figure was set alight to the satisfaction of the assembled Apprentice Boys and their supporters.

The shirt industry was, and still is, the major employer of female labour in the city. The 1957 issue of the Derry and N.W. Ireland directory listed twenty-eight shirt and collar manufacturers whilst thirty years on, only nine appeared in the Yellow Pages. In the intervening period such household names as Bryce & Weston, Hamilton, Hogg & Mitchell, Little, and Young & Rochester have disappeared from the scene.

The Atlantic Factory, Carlisle Road, was one of the smaller shirt and collar factories which were in existence during the 1930s.

A scene in W. J. Little's shirt and collar factory, Spencer Road. The premises occupied by this firm were formerly part of the Waterside Distillery complex which closed down in 1925.

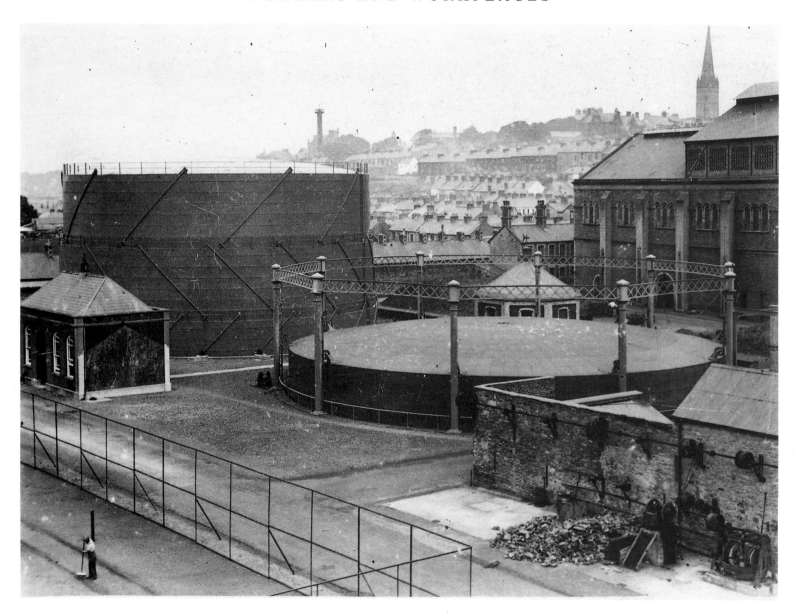

The Londonderry Gaslight Company commenced operations at Foyle Street in 1829 and as the city prospered the company moved to much larger premises in Lecky Road where it remained until its closure in the late 1980s.

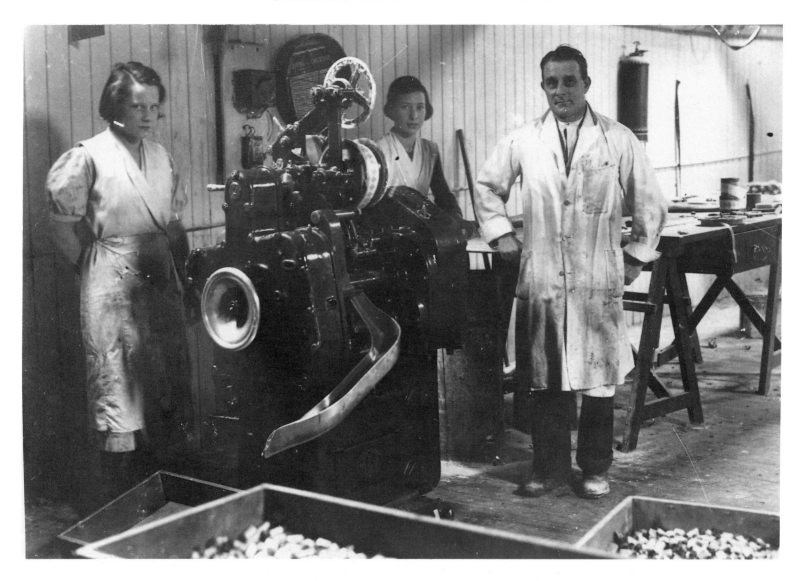

In 1933 when border restrictions reduced the bread trade to Donegal, Hugh Stevenson & Co. Ltd, of William Street, diversified by introducing a confectionery department to their bakery, and this scene shows part of the toffee making plant, which produced 'Derry Assorted' and 'Foyle Boy' toffees. In addition to the bakery the firm managed two restaurants, Stevenson's in Waterloo place and Thompson's in Ferryquay Street.

Bakers in Brewsters with a newly-baked batch of cottage loaves. The 'Important Notice' on the wall reminds staff that smoking on the premises will mean immediate dismissal.

Romain Willman, centre of the back row, with his staff of barbers and hairdressers, taken in the early 1930s. Willman's was the city's foremost hairdressing establishment and it operated from Market Buildings, Strand Road.

The apparatus was used in Willman's hairdressers, Strand Road, in the early 1930s so that ladies could have their hair 'permanently' waved.

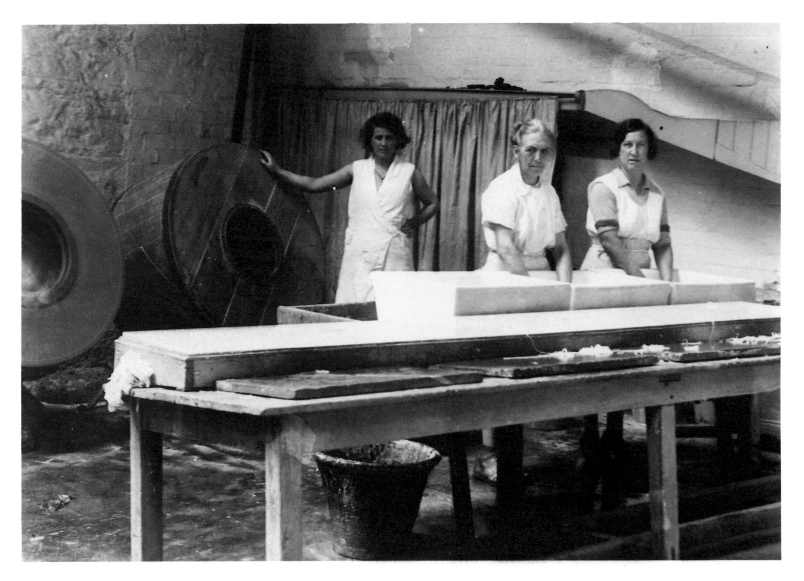

The large cylindrical container on which the woman on the left is resting her hand is a 'Dolly' which was constructed from wood and brass and used in shirt factory laundries to starch white collars. About twelve collars were threaded together on string through the stud holes and then placed in the 'Dolly' which held the starch solution. After this the container was revolved mechanically.

A square setted surface in William Street with the staff of the Castle Laundry posing in front of their new Ford Van, which was supplied by Alexander Motor Co. in adjoining Great James Street. As well as dealing with laundry from households, the firm would have carried out contract work for some of the local shirt factories.

Long and faithful service with the Post Office was rewarded with a medal from the powers-that-be and a silver service from work mates. In the second row, fifth and tenth from the left, are two 'Telegraph Boys' who delivered telegraphs containing urgent messages at a time when telephones were not so common.

In 1937 a new automatic telephone exchange was opened and the operators at the switchboard are shown here under the steely eye of the supervisor.

The staff of All Cash Stores outside the company's headquarters in Strand Road. The firm's boast was that it was the largest retailer in the North West, and at one time had over thirty branches covering an area from Portrush in Co. Antrim to St Johnston in Co. Donegal. There are 64 people in this group all of whom would have been full-time employees. The building was demolished in 1989 after having been set on fire during the present civil unrest.

James Morrison Ltd of Duke Street, was one of the largest drapers and milliners in the Waterside. One of the shop windows is shown here dressed for an 'Ulster Shopping Week' when customers were exhorted to purchase 'Goods made in Ulster'.

Edmiston & Co. Ltd in Shipquay Street was one of the leading hardware merchants which flourished in the city pre-war. As well as having the retail shop they had a wholesale section. Wallace Edmiston, the firm's founder, wearing a hat, is in the centre of the group whilst his son, Macrea, who was well known in local amateur dramatic circles, is on the extreme right. This photograph was taken prior to the staff's annual outing to Shrove, Co. Donegal, in 1939.

One of the many events in the Guildhall during the 1930s was an 'Ideal Homes Exhibition' where many of the businesses took stands. As well as operating the Rock Mills, which produced flour and meal, S. Gilliland & Sons Ltd also operated a thriving bakery which in its latter years was run by the Limavady family of Hunters.

Some fifteen years before this scene was photographed in 1935 a vastly different image would have been recorded by the camera showing a thriving shipyard which, along with the Watts Distillery and the various pork stores, meant that the city enjoyed the highest male employment in its history.

The fourth and perhaps the most successful shipyard to operate in the city was the North of Ireland Shipbuilding Co. Ltd which commenced in 1912 and closed in 1924. In the early 1920s the workforce numbered as high as 2,600. The scene depicted here was taken in the 1930s when demolition work of some of the buildings was being carried out. The large brick building in the background housed the yard's electricity station and dominated the bottom of the Strand Road until it was removed in the late 1980s.

James Harper Ltd of Duke Street were the only manufacturers of boots and shoes in the North-West. 'Shamrock' was the trade name of their products which were of high quality and enjoyed a deserved reputation, far beyond the local area.

The largest employers of male labour after the closure of the shipyard in 1924 were local pork stores. This scene of bacon being rolled would cause apoplexy to a present-day environmental health officer considering the conditions and the workers' clothing.

Foyle Street Market's official title was the Butter and Pork Market: but as changes took place in the agricultural world some of the covered accommodation was converted into stores and offices where fruit and vegetable wholesalers carried on their businesses. It also contained the Weights and Measures Office and weighbridge firm. In this scene fleeces are the main product being offered for sale.

The hiring fairs for farm workers, or the Rabbles as they were known in the North-West, took place in the Diamond twice a year on the three successive Wednesdays after the 12th May and 12th November. By the time this scene was recorded in 1937 its importance had declined to the extent that very few workers were hired and the day was more of a holiday for the rural community.

McMonagle's Long Car pictured in 1929 with a full complement of transport manager passengers at its terminus in Strand Road opposite the Lough Swilly Railway Station. The Long Car's other terminus was Waterloo Place (opposite the Northern Counties Hotel) and it served the city for 50 years, ceasing in April 1931. Mr McMonagle is standing beside the man holding the reins.

Coaches owned by R. Neely & Co., waiting at the entrance of the L.M.S. Station, Waterside, for the arrival of the assize judges who were then conveyed to their lodgings at Carlisle Terrace.

Up to the early 1950s there were numerous donkeys in the city and environs which were used to transport goods and people. This scene at Newmarket Street shows what appears to be a home-made mode of conveyance.

A happy scene at L.M.S. Station, Waterside, just as a passenger train was about to commence its journey. The only male to be seen is the engine driver, so it might not be wrong to assume the passengers are staff of a local shirt factory on the occasion of the annual outing.

Six drivers pose in front of a Leyland bus in Harbour Square. H.M.S. Catherwood was the second operator of the city's bus service and continued up to 1936 when the province-wide Northern Ireland Road Transport Board came into existence.

This 1934 scene at McCandless & Piggots' Garage, Strand Road, shows a Hillman Minx saloon car.
The notice in the showroom states that the price of the car is £159-0-0.

Hugh Stevenson & Co Ltd was one of the main bakeries in the city, and in common with a great number of business houses supported the North-West Ireland Agricultural Society's Summer Show at Brandywell by entering this decorated van which is parked here outside the firm's premises in William Street.

Donegal buttermilk carts wait for the Galliagh Road Customs Post to open. The vendors of this delectable drink had a second obstacle to surmount before making sales in the city as the Corporation levied a charge of 6d per cart which was collected on Buncrana Road inside the city boundary.

A motor van and two horse-drawn vehicles belonging to the Rock Biscuit Company on the quay immediately behind the Rock Mills, before setting out to take part in a large parade of vehicles to Brandywell Showgrounds. Note the sign on the windscreen of the van which proclaims 'Derry Built Van'.

Eight drivers, accident free for the previous twelve months, receive cheques for £5.0.0 from W. J. Porter, the owner of the All Cash Stores, outside the firm's headquarters in Strand Road. This event took place in 1939 when £5.0.0 would have been much more than the weekly wage of a van driver.

Brandywell Recreation Grounds on the occasion of the North-West of Ireland Agricultural Society's Summer Show when the local business firms entered their vehicles in a competition which was one of the attractions. The covered accommodation in which spectators are seated backed onto the Brandywell Road perimeter wall of the grounds.

William Thompson's stand in Brandywell Showgrounds on the occasion of the summer agricultural show. There is a wide variety of machinery etc. on display, including binders, reapers, a threshing mill and churns. Founded in 1825 the firm traded until the mid 1970s.

John C. Drennan of Carse Hall, Limavady, showing off his prize winning Clydesdale in Brandywell Grounds at North West Ireland Agricultural Society's Summer Show. In the background is the wooden grandstand which was replaced in the mid 1950s. There is no greyhound track in evidence in this scene.

Chamberlain Street Livestock Market was the place where farmers bought and sold their animals for over three centuries as Thomas Raven's map of 1625 describes the site as the 'Beast Markett'. In 1964 the market was transferred to Brandywell Showgrounds to allow housing re-development take place in the Lecky Road area. In the early 1970s the market was again changed to Lisahally.

Scene in the Council Chamber of the Guildhall during Sir James Wilton's tenure as Mayor (1935-39) when the Irish Society were visiting the city. The members of the Society are the line of robed men on the right. The Governor is seated on the Mayor's right.

Representatives of all parties in Londonderry Corporation join together in congratulating Sir Basil McFarland on his appointment as Mayor of the city in May 1939. He only completed five months of his term of office before going off to serve with the 9th Derry Heavy Anti-Aircraft Regiment and the post was taken over by Frederick Simmons, on the left, third row back. On sir Basil's right is Patrick Maxwell solicitor, who finished up his legal career as the very acceptable local Resident Magistrate, whilst on his left is Sir James Wilton who had served as Mayor from 1935 to 1939.

81

The Londonderry Corporation's first two mechanical street cleaning vehicles stand outside the Heysham Shed after being off-loaded from the cross-channel steamer which can be seen through the open door of the shed. The registration numbers were UI3114 and UI3115 and the one nearer the camera was a sweeper/washer, the other a sweeper/collector.

The turbine room of the Corporation's coal-fired electricity station, Strand Road, which served the city for over sixty years before the N.I. Electricity Service opened its oil-fired station at Coolkeeragh.

The Duke of Abercorn, Governor of Northern Ireland, flanked by the Mayor, James Wilton and J. Denham Corbett, Chairman of the Water Committee, and other guests at the official opening of Banagher Water Works on 19th November, 1935. Before this, the city's water sources were inadequate to cope with increasing demand, especially when there was a drought.

The scene in Shipquay Place on 15 May 1935 when the Duke of Gloucester visited the city. Harry Wilson is the officer in charge of the guard of honour which is composed of members of the 'B' Specials. Wallace Kennedy, City Commandant, is immediately behind.

The opening of the assizes provided a dash of ceremonial when a military guard of honour accompanied by a band was drawn up outside the Courthouse in Bishop Street. Here the Assize Judge bows to the colours of the Yorks and Lancashire Regiment which provided the guard of honour. The ceremony attracted quite a large crowd including a number of children, some of whom are barefoot.

Mr Justice Brown inspecting a guard of honour mounted by the R.U.C. in Carlisle Terrace. The judges lodged in No.1 Carlisle Terrace which was owned by the McCutcheon family, and were guarded by soldiers or police who occupied two sentry boxes, one of which may be seen behind the police in this scene. As Mr Justice Brown was a man of ample proportions a larger than normal bath had to be installed in the lodgings, where it still remains. The year is 1939.

The committee of the Eye, Ear and Throat Hospital in the garden of the Northland Road building. The matron, Miss Wilson, is seated on the left, whilst the Secretary, William S. Sterritt, a well-known local accountant, is on the right of the same row.

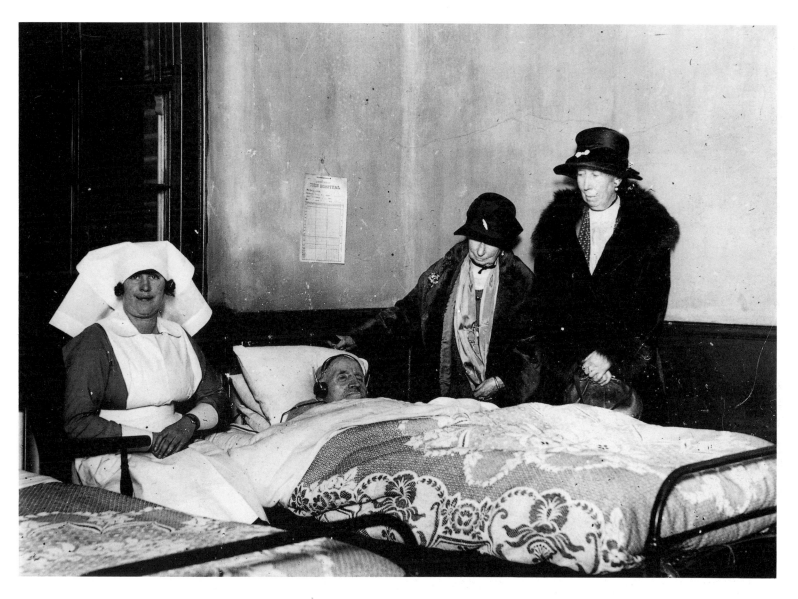

An acceptable innovation to the amenities of Waterside Hospital in the decade before the outbreak of the second world war was the introduction of radio programmes to the patients by means of headphones. No doubt the two ladies were members of the organisation which produced the funds to install the means to receive entertainment.

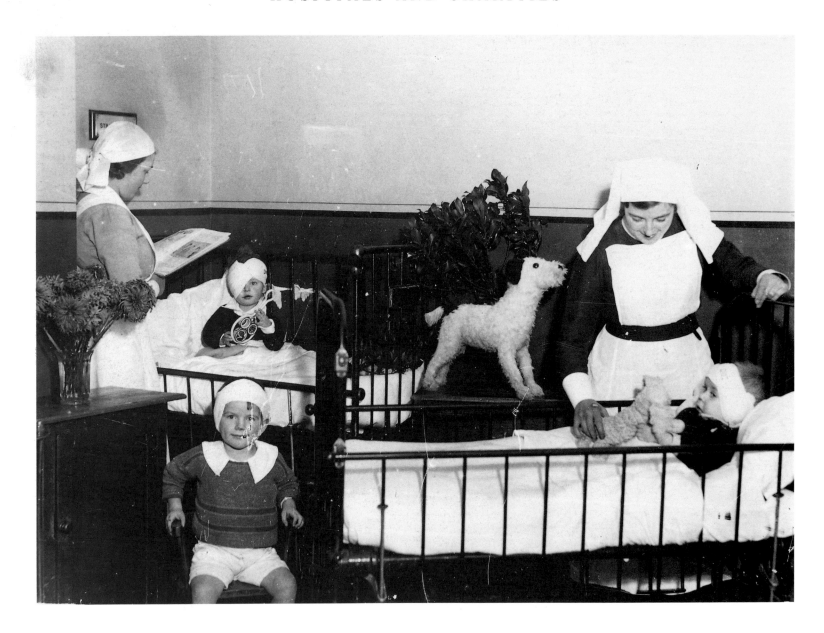

The children's ward of the Eye, Ear and Throat Hospital, Northland Road.

The only way quite a number of charitable organisations could exist was by holding fund raising events, the most popular of which was a flag day. Here lady flag sellers pose at the entrance of Ozaman House, Bridge Street, the headquarters of St Vincent De Paul Society, before fanning out into the nearby shopping arena.

As citizens of a port the people of Derry gave ready support to the charity collection which was most important to seafarers, Lifeboat Flag Day, which on this occasion was supplemented by the sale of garden produce from a flat cart at Harbour Square.

The City and County Hospital, as its name implied, catered for the residents of both town and country. The hospital depended on funds raised by various means, including flag days, one of which is recorded here in the late 1920s in Claudy Village, about 8 miles from the city.

The first talking film to be shown in the city was 'The Singing Fool' with Al Jolson taking the principal role. The venue for this momentous event was the Midland Cinema in Bond's Hill.

Before the massive loud speaker was off-loaded outside the Palace Cinema in 1929, it was driven round the main streets in order to advertise the fact that the proprietors were installing the most modern sound equipment available.

The City Cinema in William Street was one of six 'picture houses' which flourished during the 1930s. It attracted and attempted to retain the youthful patrons attending the Saturday afternoon matinees by screening an episode of a film each week, commonly known as the 'continuous', similar in purpose to the current long running 'Soap Operas' that appear on T.V.

This scene brightened up the darkness of the Strand Road and advertised the delights of the popular 1930s cinema. The Strand Cinema was the last cinema to open in the city on 24th December 1934 when it had a seating capacity of 1600: it still continues to flourish.

The staff of the Strand Cinema shortly after its opening in late 1934.

It is not often that the projection room of a cinema is photographed, but shortly after the Strand opened, this scene appeared in the *Derry Standard* as part of a report about the new picturehouse. Freddy Box, the chief projectionist, is attending the equipment on the left.

The Opera House on Carlisle Road was the best known and oldest public places of entertainment in the city which, before it was destroyed by fire in the early 1940s, showed films as well as the live shows. The show depicted here could well be 'The Desert Song'.

The cast of 'The Creaking Chair' photographed on the stage of the Opera House, Carlisle Road, in 1928. This group of local amateurs called themselves Derry Repertory Company and had a successful run for a week. On the left, standing, is Dudley E. B. McCorkell, Mayor 1929-1934, who acted the part of the butler, whilst the two men standing immediately behind the chair are E. D. R. (Don) Shearer who was Philip Speed, a journalist who turned out to be the murderer, and Patrick Macrory, later knighted, who acted the part of the hero, John Cutting. Sir Patrick alleges he was given the part because no other male member of the company was tall enough to play opposite the heroine who was, as he relates in *Days That Are Gone* 'A girl of great stature'.

101

As its name implies the Melville Band took the name of the hotel in which it originally played. It was one of the foremost dance bands in the province from the 1930s to 60s. The names of the members shown here in the Melville Hotel ballroom are, from the left:- Jack Ayling, Josie McIntyre, Fred Robinson, Willy McIntyre and Tony Black.

This early 30s scene is in Ashfield Hall, where those not roller skating were able to look on from the gallery. It would appear that the photographer placed a chalk mark on the floor beyond which the skaters were requested not to pass.

The Guildhall was the venue for what, in all probability, was advertised in the local press as a 'Monster Whist Drive.' This particular event was in aid of the funds of St Eugene's Cathedral, the Administrator of which, Fr J. Bonner, is standing on the right.

An early B.B.C. broadcast in the Minor Hall of the Guildhall showing the G.P.O. Male Voice Choir and their conductor, Redmond Friel.

An early 1930s scene in Austin's of the Diamond where mannequin parades were a regular feature of the store's attractions.

Austin's of the Diamond (The Great Clothiers) staff dance in the mid 1930s. Glover Austin is seated beside the violinist and Aldwyn Austin is seated in the centre of the second row.

A happy group of dancers in the Corinthian Ballroom, Bishop Street, participating in a set dance such as a 'Military two-step' or 'Valetta'. Prior to its adaptation to a dance hall the premises housed one of the city's leading drapery establishments, Mulholland's.

108

The scene in the Corinthian Ballroom, Bishop Street, on the occasion of the annual staff dance of Jones and Lowthers, launderers, whose business premises were situated in Bishop Street. Ernest Lowther, the proprietor, is in the centre of the seated row and the person in the dinner suit standing slightly to the right, two rows back from Mr Lowther, is Edward J. Lynch who would have acted as M.C. The bar was set up in the gentlemen's cloakroom, which meant that the ladies were deprived of buying their own liquid refreshment.

The Britannia Band originally was a flute band when it was founded in 1866, changing to brass instruments in 1875 and adding reeds prior to 1901. This photograph was taken c.1930 in the garden of the Bishop's Palace, Bishop Street. The names are:- Back row: J. Jackson, T. Heatley, Alban Goodman, J. McCauley, H. Hamill, Stewart Heatley, Geo. Simpson, Herbert C. Reynolds, Geof. Simpson. Middle row: J. McHugh, A. Campbell, A. Jackson, D. McCauley, W. Gillen, J. Currie, F. Hutchins, R.J. Harte, J. Crawford, Gerry Simpson. Seated: A. McIntyre, H. Faulkner, E. Fitzgerald, J. Rodgers, J. Wray, Geo. Orr, W. D. Aickin, Jim Goodman, (Boy G. Hutchins), T. Finlay, R. Heatley, Samuel Orr. On ground: R. Henderson.

Ist Magheramason Boy's Brigade Company was started in 1931 and is shown here shortly after its inception. Seated in the middle of the front row is the founder, Captain and Chaplain, Rev. F.W.C. Wallace, M.A.

The scene at the Great Northern Railway terminus, Foyle Road, in June 1932, before the local Catholic Boy Scouts boarded the train to Dublin where they acted as first aiders and stewards during the Eucharistic Congress. A large gathering of parents, friends and four Christian Brothers from the Brow-of-the hill came to wish them 'Bon Voyage'. The three brothers on the left are Bros Collins, Stapleton and O'Connor, whilst Bro. McGuinness is standing on the right of scouts in the front row.

The Hamilton Flute Band outside 104/106 Spencer Road in 1928 on the occasion of the presentation of new Crown AZ Rosewood flutes. In 1914 the band joined the army en-bloc as did the members of the No Surrender Band at the outbreak of the second world war in 1939. The house is now Waterside Police Station. The names in the photograph are:- Sixth row: Richard Hartin, Oswald Orr, Jack Hughes, James Pomeroy, Thomas Colhoun, Thomas Alford, James Strawbridge. Fifth row: Thomas Wright, Alex McIntyre, Hugh Buchanan, Jack Falconer, Robert Philson, Harry Hughes. Fourth row: Robert Hamill, William McClay, William Peoples, David McGarvey. Third row: Jackie Parkhill, Archie McElwee, William Kincaid, Billy Duncan. Second row: David Colhoun, Hugh McIntyre, James Blair, Herbert Andrews, Archie Heaney, Robert McClay, John McNulty, Robert Curry, William Duddy, Alex Kane. Front row: Robert Blair, ? , James Blair, Mrs Holmes, Mrs Corscadden, Mrs Graham, Dealtry Thompson, ? , Bertie Riddle, Thomas Galbraith.

St Columba's Old Oak Flute was a popular pre-war group which competed successfully in musical competitions. One of the band's possessions was a banner on which was depicted the city's Patron Saint, but unfortunately this is no longer in existence.

Four successful competitors in the solo violin competition of Féis Doire Columcille, c.1939. This event is held in the Guildhall during Easter week. The four young musicians here are:- Maisie Strickland, Daniel McLaughlin, Terence McDonald (one of the compilers of this book) and his sister Patricia.

A successful class of competitors from the Christian Brothers Primary School, Brow-of-the-hill, at the Féis Doire Columcille. The Christian Brothers came to the city in 1854 and provided free primary education which eventually was extended to include technical education as well. The order officially ended its connection with the area in 1990.

Carlisle Road Presbyterian Church Choir in the Minor Hall of the Guildhall after successfully competing in the Londonderry Féis. The minister of the church, Rev. Samuel McVicker, is on the extreme left of the back row. In his younger days he was a well-known sportsman, representing his country in hockey and rugby.

Donemana Percussion Band with its conductor, Miss Lou Hamilton, holding the cup, after having defeated 2nd Girls' Life Brigade, 1st Derry, at the Londonderry Féis in the Guildhall, March 1939. The test piece was Minuet and Chaconne (Gluck).

One of the most popular organisations in the city during the 1930s was the Londonderry Philharmonic Society whose members are shown here on the Guildhall platform. The moving spirit and conductor of the society, J. C. Cunningham, is standing on the left immediately below the organ loft.

Londonderry's Y.M.C.A. had their playing fields at Duncreggan Road which in the 20s and 30s was more popularly known as Tillie's Lane. There are only five houses in Aberfoyle Crescent as seen here in the background and it would appear that the association augmented its funds by allowing a local farmer to graze his sheep on the land. This scene was photographed in 1932 and the team is Strabane Y.M.C.A. which appears to have been lacking at least two players as JAmes Guthrie and Gilmore Smith, standing on the extreme left and right respectively, were both members of Derry Y.M.

G. Gallan leads the City of Derry senior team on to the field at Lower Duncreggan in 1939 for their semi-final cup game against Sion Mills. From the left are: F. Moore, J. Roulston (Umpire), G. Stewart, E. Gallen (Umpire), J. McClune (hidden by G. G. McClelland), E.D.R. Shearer, F. Chambers, S.l. McCombe, A.B. McCarroll, G. Morrow and J. Gallan.

City of Derry Rowing Club's coxed four about to compete in the local regatta. The steps shown in this scene were sited almost opposite the club's headquarters on the quay at the foot of Boating Club Lane. Number 3 and Bow of this crew are the Ward Brothers, Vincent and Dick.

Scene from the river during the City of Derry Rowing Club's annual regatta showing an eights race in progress with the Harbour Board's tug, T. F. Cooke, bringing up the rear. The large chimney in the foreground of the quayside is that belonging to the Corporation's coal-fired electricity station.

Men's hockey was a popular local sport up to the mid 1950s. This scene shows the action in a match at Magee University College's grounds, Duncreggan Road, in which the Londonderry Y.M.C.A. is attacking the goal in picture. Inside the circle is Thompson Jamieson, who has just hit the ball, immediately behind him, Gerald Frew, and on the right, Barry Jamieson.

Before the war, City of Derry Harriers had its headquarters in premises at Glen Road where cross-country competitions started and where this group was photographed.

The Londonderry Rotary Club's golf competition at Castlerock in the early 1930s. Standing fourth and fifth from the left in the second row and fourth on the third row are Jack Colhoun, Samuel Dowds and Albert Anderson, who all served as mayors of the city in the 50s and 60s.

The combined rugby teams of Waterside and Derry prior to their annual match for the Foyle Challenge Cup Match on Saturday, 19th March, 1931 at Rectory Field, Limavady Road. Sir Basil A.T. McFarland was the referee with A. W. Anderson, captain of the Waterside team, and R. G. Bennett, captain of the Derry side. Waterside won 20-13. The following names appear in the *Standard's* report of the match:- McRitchie, Glover, McClure, Walker, Moreton, Cochrane, A. W. Anderson, R. N. Anderson, Elliot, Sidebottom, Magill, McCandless, McCullagh and McLaughlin.

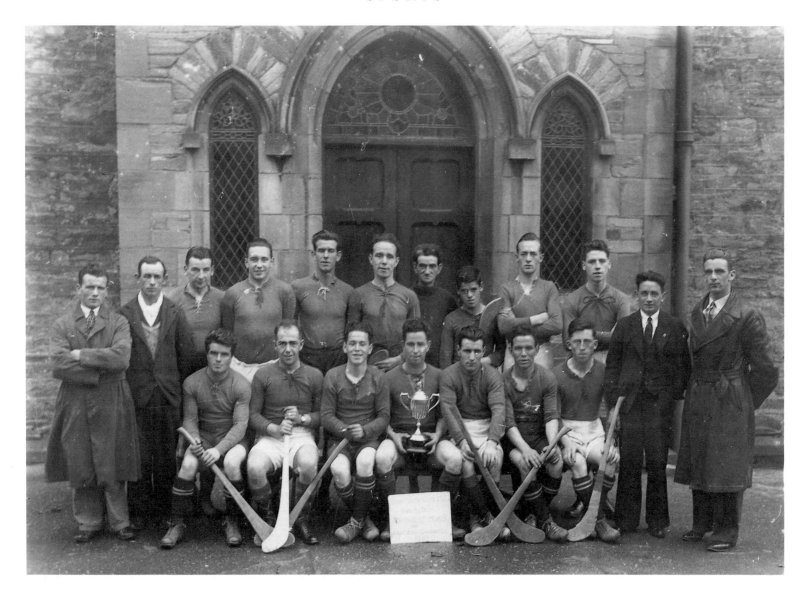

Whilst hurling never enjoyed the same popularity as association football, it had, and still has, a keen following in the city. Here the Young Sarsfields Hurling Club pose outside St Eugene's School, Francis Street, after winning the North-West League and Derry County Championship during the 1933-4 season.

Pre-season training at Brandywell in 1936 on a pitch from which it would appear a crop of hay is about to be cut. The players are, left to right, unknown, P. Nelis, Bobby Browne, Ashley Hobson, John McCurran, John Smith (Buncrana), Jimmy McCann, Willie Healey, Matt Doherty, unknown at back, Fred Mason and Jack Common.

An early scene in Brandywell Grounds after senior football came to the city when Derry City F.C. played in the Aston Villa colours of claret and blue shirts and white shorts. In this scene there is no covered accommodation in the unreserved side and no houses immediately adjacent to the perimeter fence.

A packed house at Brandywell during the mid 1930s. Edward Lynch is seated outside the wooden fence with his youthful assistants round him. They sold programmes and tickets for a draw which took place at half-time.

When greyhound racing commenced at Brandywell Grounds in the early 1930s these followers of the sport advertised the fact by parading their dogs through the main streets of the city, and are photographed here outside the *Derry Standard* premises in Shipquay Street. Holding the leash of the black dog in the centre of the group is Jimmy 'Spider' Kelly, the well-known local professional boxer.

A scene at Brandywell Grounds greyhound racetrack shortly after racing started up. The building in the background is the wheelhouse where the speed of the hare is controlled.

Brooke Park Bowling Green was officially opened on 23rd June 1928 when Lady McFarland was
the recipient of a replica bowl-topped walking stick. On her left is the Mayor, James Hamilton, who
was the proprietor of a thriving shirt and collar factory in John Street.

Bowls was a late-comer in the sporting life of the city. The corporation provided a green at Brooke Park where City of Derry Bowling Club and a visiting team pose, c. 1935.

Badminton during the 1930s was a popular indoor, winter sport which was enjoyed by players of varied ability. Perhaps the four best exponents of the game in the north-west, all of whom represented their country, were:- Jim Rankin, Thomas Orr, Thomas Henry and Hugh (Budge) Montgomery.

Scene in the billiards and snooker room of the Presbyterian Working Men's Institution, The Diamond. The players are W. J. (Jim) Denning on the left and Michael Doherty of Chamberlain Street, on the right, two of the best exponents of billiards in the north-west for many years.

City of Derry Wheelers at Limavady Road during the 1930s. Limavady Road was the usual venue where the Wheelers held their competitions.

St John's Ambulance Brigade personnel are shown here at Brandywell Grounds where they attended to injuries or sudden illness during sporting events. Third from the left of the back row is William Ward who was the proprietor of the well-known monumental sculptors who operated from premises at the junction of John Street and Foyle Road; he also served on the management committee of the City and County Hospital.

Amelia Earhart's plane 'Friendship' in the field at Springfield where it made a dramatic landing on 21st May 1932. In reply to interviewers' questions in London a few days later, Miss Earhart declared, 'I had made up my mind to fly alone, because if there is a man in the machine you can bet your life he wants to take control'. The plane was a Lockheed Vega aircraft.

Amelia Earhert, the first female to fly the Atlantic solo, pictured in the doorway of Robert Gallagher's house, Springfield, after her eventful flight on 20/21 May, 1932. The distance covered was 2026 miles which took 13 1/4 hours.

General Balbo with members of the local Italian Community at Harbour Square during the visit of the massed flight of seaplanes from Rome en route to Chicago in July 1933. During the war he was Governor of Libya and when he was coming in to land at his own airfield, Italian gunners shot down his plane.

Army recruiting marches through the city were a common sight during the twenties and thirties and attracted a large number of young men and boys. One such march is depicted here, as a detachment of soldiers, headed by a small band, enters the Diamond from Shipquay Street. The band in this instance is made up of pipers from the Royal Inniskilling Fusiliers and Royal Irish Fusiliers.

William McGahey's funeral passing the gaol in Bishop Street, on its way to the City Cemetery in May 1933. The turret in this scene is the only part of the building which was retained when the Fountain Street area was redeveloped in the early 1970s and indeed everything else outside the walls in this scene has been demolished. William McGahey was the Sergeant-Major in the 10th Inniskillings during the 1914-18 War and was stationed in Dublin during the 1916 Rising when he used his influence to prevent unnecessary bloodshed.

This wheeled sandwich board was a common sight in the city and its owner Edward J. (Hawker) Lynch was one of the best known characters in the city from the late twenties up to his death in 1965. Hawker had a quick wit and it was a brave man who bandied words with him. On one occasion when Derry City was playing Linfield at Brandywell a supporter of the latter team attempted to get the better of him. Eddy's retort was 'Derry, Aughrim, Enniskillen and the Boyne - your wee village wasn't even mentioned!'.

A Lancia with armed police sets off across Carlisle Bridge with its load of ballot boxes for delivery to polling stations for an election.

Most speakers at the Rotary Club would not have warranted a photograph being taken for insertion in the *Derry Standard*; but when the quest was Sir Basil Brooke (later Lord Brookeborough) the Minister of Agriculture, then such was the case. The headline of the report in the paper on 22nd February 1939 was "Sir Basil Brooke's address in Derry-Solving the Farmers' problems". The President is John A. Crockett of Crockett & Guy, Hardware Merchants, Strand Road.

The children of the Fountain Street area had a readymade playground on the city walls at Church
Wall, where Tommy Holmes is shown here throwing a marble.

The choristers of St Columb's Cathedral c.1935 at the War Memorial on Armistice Day. They are led by John T. Frankland, Organist and Master of the Choristers from 1921 to his death in 1948. He was described as 'A stern disciplinarian who would brook no nonsense from anyone . . .' Fifty-five years later Leslie Laverty, on the left holding the music at knee level, is still an active member of the choir.

A well stocked bar where one could order stout from a crockery bottle which would be a collectors' item. The glass hatch on the right enabled patrons who were in the snug to order their drinks. The cat on top of the wooden partition appears to be as interested in having its photograph taken as the barman.

Charles George O'Brien (1876-1942), one of the characters in the city during the 1930s, is pictured here on the Branch Road where Foyle and Londonderry College's playing fields are at present. Before becoming a little eccentric he was a solicitor and one of his nicknames was 'Walk-a-bike', as he was never known to ride his bicycle. There are many stories told about Charles George, most of them apocryphal; but almost fifty years after his death he is remembered with affection.

The local Italian community formed itself into a Fascistii, the men of which were known as 'Black Shirts'. On the wall in the centre, is a photograph of 1L Duce, Mussolini, flanked by the King and Queen of Italy. The man not in uniform holding the violin is Orlando Cafolla, the well-known musician and teacher.

The provision of a meal for members of the Black Shirts would have presented no problem to any of the men shown here as most of them were involved in the catering industry, and it would be no exaggeration to say that most of the city's fish and chip shops and ice cream parlours were owned by the local Italian community. On the table H.P. sauce appears incongruous alongside bottles of Chianti.

There was a sizeable number of Scots resident in the city pre-war who played an active part in its life, as well as coming together to honour their national poet on Burn's Night. The two men nearest the camera on the right are more interested in the menu than having their photograph taken.

There was poverty in the city in the 1930s which was alleviated in some small measure by the provision of 'Penny Dinners'. The man and boys seated at the right are quite willing to have their photographs taken; but the girl on the left is unwilling to face the camera.

The scene outside St Columb's Cathedral after the wedding of William Henry (Harry) Platt and Mary Wilhelmina Walker on 14th September 1933. The names are:- standing left to right: John Walker, James Boal, William Walker, Bertie Platt, Nettie Finlay, John C. Love, Raymond Platt, Hubert Platt, Harry Platt, Jean Walker; seated:- Kathleen Boal, Catherine Platt, Avril Platt, bride and groom, Samuel Taggart, Margaret A. Walker, Katthleen Love; seated on rug:- Angus R. M. Platt, Desmond N. O. Boal, Kathleen Boal, Maureen Boal.

Diana Watchman and Sydney W. Shaw of Glasgow after their wedding in the Jewish Synagogue, Kennedy Place, in August 1939.

The scene in the City Hotel after the wedding of Robert J. Cumings, Belfast, and Cissie O'Doherty of Magazine Street, in St Columba's church, Long Tower, in September 1935. The celebrants at the Nuptial Mass were Most Rev. J. R. Mageean, Bishop of Down and Connor (uncle of the groom), and Fr Daniel Cumings C.S.S.R. (brother of the groom). The bestman was Robert McGouran and the groomsman was William George O'Doherty. The bridesmaids were Rosie O'Doherty and Margaret Cumings.

Firemen provided a guard of honour at Claremont Presbyterian Church when the City's Fire Chief, Peter Gaylor, was married to a Frances Ferguson on 6th February 1933.

When war broke out in September 1939 the citizens were issued with gas masks which were fitted
by members of the police, as shown in this scene at the yard of L.M.S. Railway Station, Waterside.

The scene in Limavady Road on Saturday, November 4th 1939, when the 9th (Londonderry), Heavy Anti-aircraft Regiment, Royal Artillery, marched from Caw Camp, led by the band of the South Wales Borderers to the Midland Station where they left the city on board the 4.30 p.m. train for Larne. Capt. Sir Basil McFarland is at the head of the 25th Battery with Lt Emerson H. Babington behind. The sergeant in the front row, left, is MaCrea Edmiston.

ACKNOWLEDGEMENTS

The compilers wish to record their thanks to the undernoted without whose help, unstintingly given, this would have been a much poorer offering.

Maureen Boal

William Coulter

Jim Denning

Norman Doherty

Richard Doherty

William Dougherty

Jack Elliott

William Ferguson

Charles Gallagher

Jim Goodman

Fred Logan

Thomas Maguire

Nano McCabe

David McDaid

Robert McGilloway

Rev. E.G. McKimmon

Rev. E.S. McKinney

Donald O'Doherty

Very Rev. D.S. Orr

Thomas Orr

Arthur Willman

William Wright

BIBLIOGRAPHY

Brian Bonner, *Derry - An outline history of the diocese*, Dublin, 1982.

A.A. Campbell, *Belfast Naturalists' Field Club: its origins and progress*, Belfast, 1938.

Col. Colby ed., Ordnance survey of the County of Londonderry Vol. 1, Dublin, 1837.

Derry Standard, *Derry & N.W. Directory 1957*, Derry, 1985.

Richard Doherty, *Wall of Steel*, Limavady, 1988.

Charles Gallagher, *Acorns and oakleaves - A Derry childhood*, Derry, 1981.

Jim Goodman and Ian Bartlett, *Britania Band, Londonderry 1866-1985*.

R.F.G. Holmes, *Magee, 1865-1965*, Derry 1965.

Sam Hughes, *City on the Foyle*, Derry, 1985.

C.D. Milligan, *History of the siege of Londonderry*, Derry, 1951.

Brian Mitchell, *On the banks of the Foyle*, Belfast 1989.

J. F. McCartney, *Pennyburn*, Derry, 1984.

E.B. McGuire, *Irish whiskey -a history of distilling in Ireland*, Dublin, 1973.

D.B. McNeill, *Irish passenger steamship services, Vol. 1. North of Ireland*, Newton Abbott, 1969.

Patrick Macrory, *Days that are gone*, Limavady, 1983.

W.H.W. Platt, *N.W. of Ireland Cricket Union Centenary Brochure*, Derry, 1988.

W.H.W. Platt, *N.W. Senior Cricket, 1888-1968*, Derry 1968.

W.H.W. Platt, *History of Derry City Football and Athletic Club, 1929-72*. Coleraine, 1986.

Souvenir booklet of opening of Craigavon Bridge, 1933. Derry, 1933.

Souvenir of centenary of Edmund Ignatius Rice, 1844-1944, Derry, 1944.

St Columb's Cathedral historical guide, 1938,1970, Derry.

George Sweeney, *Hiring fairs in Derry, Tyrone and Donegal*, Derry, 1985.

John Turner et al, *Magheramason presbyterian church-100 years of a church and its people*, Magheramason, 1978.